Betsy Ross and the Creation of the American Flag

Kirsten Urwin

NEW YORK

Published in 2016 by The Rosen Publishing Group, Inc.
29 East 21st Street, New York, NY 10010

Photo Credits: Cover SuperStock/Getty Images; p. 4 David David Gallery/SuperStock; p. 5 Lambert/Archive Photos/
Getty Images; pp. 6, 11, 17 © North Wind Picture Archives; p. 7 Library of Congress Prints and Photographs
Division; p. 9 Archive Photos/Getty Images; p. 12 Kean Collection/Archive Photos/Getty Images; p. 13 Stock
Montage/Archive Photos/Getty Images; p. 14 Evans/Hulton Archive/Getty Images; p. 15 Hulton Archive/Archive
Photos/Getty Images; p. 18 Brown University Library, Providence, Rhode Island, USA/Bridgeman Images; p. 19
Universal Images Group/Getty Images; p. 21 Olivier Le Queinec/Shutterstock.com

Library of Congress Cataloging-in-Publication Data

Urwin, Kirsten.
 Betsy Ross and the creation of the American flag / Kirsten Urwin. -- First edition.
   pages cm. -- (Spotlight on American history)
 Includes bibliographical references and index.
 ISBN 978-1-4994-1792-0 (library bound) -- ISBN 978-1-4994-1789-0 (pbk.) -- ISBN 978-1-4994-1787-6
(6-pack)
 1. Ross, Betsy, 1752-1836--Juvenile literature. 2. Revolutionaries--United States--Biography--Juvenile literature.
3. United States--History--Revolution, 1775-1783--Flags--Juvenile literature. 4. Flags--United States--History--
18th century--Juvenile literature. I. Title.
 E302.6.R77U75 2016
 973.3092--dc23
 [B]
                                        2015018595

Manufactured in the United States of America

CPSIA Compliance Information: Batch #WS15PK: For Further Information contact Rosen Publishing, New York, New York at 1-800-237-9932

CONTENTS

THE EARLY LIFE OF BETSY ROSS. 4

THE AMERICAN REVOLUTIONARY WAR. 10

BETSY ROSS MAKES THE FIRST
AMERICAN FLAG 12

THE BRITISH ENTER PHILADELPHIA 16

THE REVOLUTIONARY WAR ENDS. 18

THE POWER OF BETSY ROSS'S STORY 22

GLOSSARY 23

INDEX 24

PRIMARY SOURCE LIST .24

WEBSITES 24

THE EARLY LIFE OF BETSY ROSS

Betsy Ross is both a **symbol** and a real person. Many people believe that Betsy Ross made the first American flag. But no one knows for sure. Whether or not she did, Betsy Ross was an unusual woman for her time.

She was born Elizabeth Griscom on January 1, 1752. Her nickname was Betsy. She lived with her family in West Jersey, Pennsylvania. There were 17 children in the Griscom family. Betsy was number eight. Her

This 18th-century painting is of a street scene in Philadelphia, Pennsylvania. It was painted on a wood panel by an unknown artist.

Henry Mosler was an artist and illustrator who lived from 1841 to 1920. In this painting, he shows Betsy Ross and her assistants sewing the first American flag.

family moved to Philadelphia when she was two years old. Later, after she married for the first time, she became known as Betsy Ross. This is the name that has become famous in American history. It is the name of an American **patriot** responsible for creating the country's most important symbol. Because of her role in making the American flag, she has become a symbol herself.

The Griscoms were Quakers. Quakers believed in simple living. They did not believe in fighting or in war. Quakers refused to fight in the French and Indian War, which lasted from 1754 until 1763. They refused to fight against the Native Americans with whom they had treaties.

Quaker children did not play cards, listen to music, or dance. They could play hide-and-seek and jump rope.

Most girls in colonial times could not go to school. But Quaker girls did. At the Quaker school, Betsy learned to read, write, and sew. She learned to sew clothes and quilts. Pennsylvania was a **colony** where the Quakers were free to practice their beliefs.

This hand-colored woodcut shows a Quaker meeting in Philadelphia in the 1800s.

The Free Quaker Meeting House at 500 Arch Street in Philadelphia, Pennsylvania, was founded in 1783. Free Quakers, including Betsy Ross, supported the American Revolution and were ready to fight for the cause of freedom.

In 1764, Betsy finished school. She was 12 years old. In that year, her father, Samuel Griscom, moved his family to a house he had built in Philadelphia.

Betsy became an **apprentice** in an **upholstery shop**. Betsy lived and worked there. In time Betsy learned to sew curtains and upholster chairs.

John Ross was also an apprentice in the same shop. Betsy and John fell in love. They married on November 4, 1773. They opened their own upholstery shop.

Quakers did not allow their members to marry people from other religions. John Ross was not a Quaker. Betsy's family was very angry when she married John. Quaker law said Betsy could no longer pray in the Quaker meetinghouse. Betsy was a strong and independent woman. She and John Ross decided to attend Christ Church. John Ross's father was a minister there. George Washington also went to Christ Church to worship. The three became friends, and Betsy sewed shirts for George Washington.

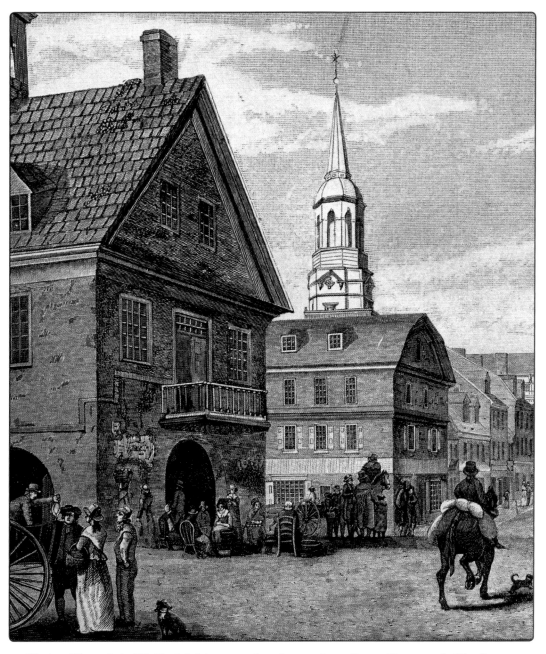

Christ Church in Philadelphia was the place where Betsy Ross probably first met George Washington. This engraving shows a view of Christ Church from Market Street in 1790. The engraving was made by William Russell Birch.

THE AMERICAN REVOLUTIONARY WAR

Soon after John and Betsy were married on November 4, 1773, Paul Revere came to Philadelphia. He told everyone that citizens in Boston had protested against a new British **tax**. A group called the Sons of Liberty had dressed as Mohawk Indians. They had climbed onto ships carrying British tea. They threw the tea into Boston Harbor. This protest was called the Boston Tea Party.

Betsy and John Ross supported the colonists who were against the British. Many Quaker men and women were patriots.

The problems between Britain and the American colonists grew. War broke out in 1775. The first battles of the American **Revolutionary War** were the Battles of Lexington and Concord on April 19, 1775.

John Ross joined the Pennsylvania militia. He guarded gunpowder. When it exploded, he was badly hurt. His wife, Betsy, nursed him but he died on January 21, 1776.

Betsy was now a **widow**. She decided to run the upholstery business that she and John had worked so hard to build. She decided to run the shop alone.

This hand-colored woodcut shows minutemen fighting in the Battle of Lexington in 1775.

BETSY ROSS MAKES THE FIRST AMERICAN FLAG

George Washington was chosen to lead the Continental army. He was the commander in chief of all the American soldiers. The army used a red and white striped flag. A small British flag was in the corner. When the British saw the flag, they thought the Americans wanted to **surrender**. Washington decided the colonies needed a new flag. The flag would

The Grand Union flag of 1776 is shown in this illustration. This was the first flag used by the colonies to symbolize their unity in the War of Independence.

This color engraving is of the American merchant and politician Robert Morris (1734–1806). Morris was a member of the Continental Congress, a signer of the Declaration of Independence, and founder of the Bank of North America.

show everyone that the Americans would fight for freedom. It would be an important symbol for patriots.

In June 1776, soon after Betsy's husband died, Betsy had a meeting with George Washington. He brought the other members of the flag committee. They were George Ross and Robert Morris. Robert Morris was very rich. He gave a lot of money to General Washington and the army. George

Ross was a relative of Betsy's late husband. He was also a member of the Continental Congress. They went to Betsy's shop with an idea for the first American flag. It had thirteen stars, one for each colony. The stars had six points. Betsy suggested using stars with five points. They liked her idea very much.

They asked her to make the flag. Betsy was very proud that these three great men trusted her with this important work.

This illustration imagines the meeting when Betsy Ross presented her design for the first American flag to George Washington, George Ross, and Robert Morris.

Betsy Ross Flag 1777

This illustration shows the American seamstress Betsy Ross sewing the first American flag adopted by the congress.

Ross's flag had seven red stripes and six white stripes. This is the same number of stripes as the flag today. She also sewed 13 white five-pointed stars on a blue background. Ross finished the work at the end of June 1776.

THE BRITISH ENTER PHILADELPHIA

In 1777, Betsy married Joseph Ashburn, a sailor. He was often at sea. Betsy ran the shop. She had a lot of work making flags for different military groups of the American army and navy.

Battles were getting close to Philadelphia. In September 1777, the British entered Philadelphia. Many businesspeople shut down their shops and left the city. But Betsy Ross stayed to protect her house and business.

British soldiers took whatever they wanted from the colonists. Soldiers even moved into Betsy's house.

In 1778, the French entered the American war against the British. The British were afraid the French might attack New York City. On June 18, 1778, the British left Philadelphia to guard New York.

In 1779, Betsy and Joseph's first daughter was born. Her name was Zillah. The next year, Joseph left to get war supplies. Soon after, Betsy had another daughter, named Eliza.

The engraving shown here is from the 1770s. It shows British soldiers living in an American colonist's home. They were clearly not welcome guests.

THE REVOLUTIONARY WAR ENDS

In October 1781, the British surrendered to the Americans at Yorktown. John Claypoole returned from England. He had been a **prisoner** of war with Joseph, Betsy's husband. The prison they were in, Old Mill Prison, was in Plymouth, England. He told Betsy of the harsh living conditions there. Betsy's second husband died in this prison. Many other American prisoners died there, too.

A watercolor by Henry de Gueydon provides a view inside Old Mill Prison at Plymouth, England.

This postcard of Betsy Ross's house was created in 1914. The Betsy Ross House at 239 Arch Street, in Philadelphia, Pennsylvania, is open to the public.

John Claypoole and Betsy became good friends. He was also a Quaker. They were married in 1783. John helped Betsy run the upholstery shop. Together they had five daughters.

John and Betsy were married for a long time. They were always very busy. They did a lot of work for the government of Pennsylvania.

John Claypoole was often sick. He had lived through the winter at Valley Forge. He survived prison in England. Betsy Ross supported the family. In June 1812, America was again at war with Britain. Betsy made a good living making flags for the American military. John Claypoole died in August 1817. Betsy was now a widow for the third time.

Betsy retired in 1827. She was 75 years old. Her daughter and a niece ran the shop. Betsy lived with another daughter.

Betsy Ross died on January 30, 1836. She was 84 years old. She lived longer than most women in America at that time. She had lived through the birth of the American nation. She created its most important symbol.

This photo is of the Betsy Ross House today. It is an important tourist landmark in the Old City of Philadelphia, Pennsylvania.

THE POWER OF BETSY ROSS'S STORY

We don't know for certain that Betsy Ross sewed the first flag. We do know that she was an independent and courageous woman. She faced difficulties with resilience. She owned her own business. She helped the American Revolution and the American army and navy. We know for certain that she was a true American patriot.

Betsy Ross had often told her family how she made the first American flag. In 1870, her grandson and other relatives told Betsy's story to the Historical Society of Pennsylvania. There is no other **proof**.

Today you can visit Betsy Ross's house at 239 Arch Street in Philadelphia. It is now a museum.